Breach

poems by

Bridget Gage Dixon

Finishing Line Press
Georgetown, Kentucky

Breach

ACKNOWLEDGMENTS

Breach originally appeared in *Drunk Monkeys*
Pluvial originally appeared in *Young Ravens Review*
The Art of Camouflage originally appeared in *Inkwell*
First Smoke originally appeared in *Anderbo*
Upon Reading that the Gene for Night Owls is Called Cry1 originally
appeared in *River Heron*
Birth originally appeared in *New York Quarterly*
Finale originally appeared in *Poetry Super Highway*
Absolution originally appeared in *Crack the Spine*

For my sister Elizabeth who gave me a blank book when I was ten and told
me to fill it with all the wanderings of my mind. Finally I'm giving one back
to you.

Publisher: Leah Huete de Maines
Editor: Christen Kincaid
Cover Art: Robert D. Dixon
Author Photo: Robert D. Dixon
Cover Design: Elizabeth Maines McCleavy

Order online: www.finishinglinepress.com
also available on amazon.com

Author inquiries and mail orders:
Finishing Line Press
PO Box 1626
Georgetown, Kentucky 40324
USA

Table of Contents

This is the Hour of Lead—
Remembered, if outlived,
As Freezing persons, recollect the Snow—
First—Chill—then Stupor—then the letting go

—Emily Dickinson

Birth

It was my mother's first betrayal-
The strain of her body against mine,
the industry of expanding bone,
as she labored to expel me
in a flood of blood and water.
The cord, twisted into a noose,
wrapped tighter every time the walls
of her womb constricted.
Nurses tilted the gurney,
hoisted my mother's feet to the ceiling,
the doctor reached in to slip the umbilical
from my neck, wrenched me from her, the sharp
edge of air against my blue-black skin,
the room suspended in the tug between
silence and the struggle for breath.

Breach

Like glass shattered by the flight of a stone,
a girl breaks beneath the weight of her grandfather.
She loves him. He is good.
He smells of hickory smoke and berries.
This smile is unfamiliar, in his palm he holds
a wildflower, she can't name it but it's beautiful.
A gift for a girl special to no one.
She moves like a ghost in a crowded house,
a small shadow in the silence of herself.
He opens his palm to offer the flower,
petals bent, stem removed.
She reaches into his palm,
spreads herself open to his hand.
For a moment she matters to someone
for a moment her body breaks open
like glass bursting at the touch of a flying stone.

The Art of Camouflage

It's an art you practiced playing kick the can on summer nights,
learning to conceal yourself before the tap
of aluminum against asphalt.

You taught yourself to crouch behind tree trunks,
tuck in beside the wheel-well of a van,
to be safe required a kind of expertise
so you counted along, lips mutely forming numbers,

seven, eight, nine, here I come.
You'd bide your time as whoever was it
headed off in some other direction
waiting for the moment when you'd sprint back
kick the dented can with your canvas sneakers.

You were safe as long as you were unseen,
 a skill you learned first under blankets,
your father's voice booming up the stairs,
doors slamming, drywall giving way beneath his heavy fists.

Your mother knew it too, practiced it with spackle and sandpaper,
she'd kneel beside the hole and spread the compound
with a dull blade, she kept a quart of paint to match every
room beneath the basement steps.

You'd watch her use her thumbnail
to break loose the last bits of plaster clinging
to the knife, see her conceal each mark
with a two-inch paintbrush.

You watched people come and go,
stood beside your Aunt Lisa as she drank her tea,
your grandfather as he ate birthday cake,
you stood right beside the welted wall
when your Nana patted you on the cheek

and you cursed each of them for not noticing
the host of small lesions, conspicuous circles
covered with slightly brighter paint.

The Divergence of Clouds

We practiced their names,
such foreign things, hefty
in our small mouths: cumulus,
cirrus, and stratus.

Backs pressed into those blades of grass
we searched their silhouettes
for what stays concealed,
our eyes rode the curved lines
smeared over blue sky.

We were believers then in the beauty
of what obscures itself, too eager
to summon metamorphosis.
Here a bear emerges,
there a mermaid,
the world was full of mysterious magic.

We learned to ride the steep black
spines of mountains
acquiring new names:
Mammatus, nimbus, cumulonimbus,
loosing themselves of burdens
their liberation a steady drumbeat
thwacking the metal roof.

But you tired of our secret sorcery,
acquired a more serviceable vocabulary:
terra firma, dividend, equilibrium,
words that slog the synapses
devoid of mysticism.

I lurched toward lyricism:
Noctilucent, flammagenitus,
Lenticular, trekked the steep
angles of imagination, the places
where clouds burn over the desert,
encircle mountain peaks, sweet haloes,
that divide darkness from day.

Fugue

Black sky dangles above the thin bones
of a garden trellis, on a chaise beneath it
you curl your spine to meet the knees
you've folded against your chest,
all your life you've tucked tragedy
into your pockets, secrets moldering
just out of sight.

Your hands, clasped, are covered
by a constellation of blue veins
memory, an unrelenting maelstrom,
thunders through you, a swift, sharp strike
to split persistent shadows.

There are words you cannot
bring your tongue to form,
a hundred wasps you've swallowed
they drone inside your throat.
You press them, when possible,
into your pleated heart, in the empty space
between each rib.

You look up through the maze of pole and wire,
past the lines that grid the heavens,
through the tarnish of streetlamp,
you can almost see the boy you were
before the sky split open,
before moon went blind,
back when god survived.

Finale

Old age should burn and rave at close of day
—Dylan Thomas

Two days before he died, just past midnight,
 grandfather rose from the spittle-soaked sheets
of a second-hand deathbed.
With cancer-gnawed hands
clawed rusted metal rails, pulled
his wasting six-foot frame to standing,
crossed the pitch-black hall to slide his palm
across the gullet of his shotgun.

He lumbered over hardwoods cursing
took aim at passing shadows.
Women crouched muttering prayers
into shuddering hands until as quickly as he'd risen
he slumped, the trail of his sweat-soaked tee-shirt
drawn across the kitchen wall.

He pitched onto his side, chest lurching as he fought for breath.
The gun slipped from his grip, fell to the floor
with a rippling thud. My mother and grandmother
threw his flaccid arms across their shoulders,
struggled with the weight of his wilting,
hauled him back to bed and returned
the hushed custodians of a weary hunter.

First Smoke

On the front seat of his father's Chevy
I slid that cigarette between my lips.
He drew the lighter from his jeans
rolled a thumb across the notched barrel,

and brought the flame to me.
His hand fumbling up my thigh,
I arched my back the way
I'd seen it done in movies I watched

while my parents slept. Even then,
struggling not to cough as smoke
slid over my tongue, down my throat,
I would not have called it love.

I only cared how long I could
hold that breath before it would
slide back out, leaving me dizzy
with the poison of it. His smoke

spun out smoothly, spread across
the sagging cloth ceiling over our heads,
each small circle he exhaled hanging there,
signals neither of us could read.

In the Winter of 86

I began to disassemble myself:
thin veil of flesh over bone,
green eye and pale pink lip,
I peeled and plucked away my youth
in hospital hallways.

Ten trembling fingers lifted pills,
placed them on dry tongue
washed the faulty communion of cure
down with the lukewarm water
from a paper cup.

Tablets dissolved in bitter acid.
Blood thick with betrayal traveled
veins that traversed limbs.
Under sallow skin tiny rivulets
teemed and pulsed with poison.

My muscles braced against invaders,
stiffened, twisted, left me a body
warped beneath the weight
of expertise.

All winter I consumed capsules
passed from busy hands, questions
parsed on barbed tongue,
dissected myself one
secret at a time.

In the Dayroom

In the dayroom they plan their escape
as a smoky mantle dances in fluorescent light.
A poet extends an arm, peels back graying gauze,
Exposes the scabbing kiss of blade on skin.

In the corner chair, a girl rapt in silence
Rocks on a lumpy canvas chair.
All around her traumas are exchanged
like tarnished coins.

The nurse etches notes in her blue binder,
orderlies troll the halls for strays.
By the window, a woman,
still in a suit speaks to the air
which answers.

The day has begun to extract its demands,
 the elixir of shared secrets, the salt of solace.
There will doctors, duties, the dirge of memory,
but for now, they suckle cigarettes, stare
at the skyline through a barricade
of smoke-glazed glass.

In the Dream

You are balanced on a railroad trellis
Far below you the river screams,
 thrashes the shore. In the distance
the faint ghost of a ship dissolves
into the horizon.

You feel certain you should not be here,
struggle to recall train schedules,
arrivals and departures, the complex math
of route and destination, you're fairly sure
you aren't safe.

In this dream you have no wings,
no feathers sprouting from your scapula
to save you when the track begins to shudder.
You realize this suddenly as the steely shriek
of the horn splits the soft Spring afternoon.

Of course, the train is black, coal-fired,
A stream of angry smoke trailing behind it,
 the kind of train you've seen only in museums
or old movies, but there it is chugging through your sleep.

There you stand between collision and collapse,
panicked, wingless, and then suddenly awake.

The Long Ride Back

She'd give her right arm to understand
the language of birds, the song of wind
as it cuts itself against cliff.

He'd surrender an eye to know
how to coax melody from misery,
ease peace from strings by fingering frets.

They stumble through the punctual bliss
of responsibility mutely managing
the weight of limbs.

The taxi sails through a red light.
An angry horn demands justice.
She stares into the narrowing horizon.
He drifts away on guitar licks.

She Says

That she understands the language of birds,
that she hears blue jays call out for higher branches,
mockingbirds for an unmolested nest-
that she understands the song the wind
sings as it stirs the limbs of trees,
that the world is full of disappointed deer.

I say take your medicine,
This is best for you, that cures
are often pulled from plants
that sacrifice themselves for you
and besides the birds prefer their privacy
the geese resent your eavesdropping.

She says the world won't listen
and the pills make her fat,
that she'd rather spend the day
gossiping with the grass
than telling her secrets to the doctor
and his notepad, that last time
she could hear the ghost of the tree whimpering
with every word he spread across the page.

I say you aren't fat,
The doctor wants to help,
stretch out my hand, three pills
nesting in my palm,
say imagine feeling normal,
she says **I do,**
and swats my hand away.

Dear Sunny,

This morning's paper, thick with the news of your death, stains my hands. Even as the black ink of the headline settles into the grooves of my fingertips, I am glad for you.

Beside your smiling photo, another of your old Toyota parked beside the tracks, a ribbon of yellow tape strains against the breeze, the train halted eternally by the camera's shocked lens and you in the distance beneath the blanket finally at rest.

The headline reads GIRL LEAPS INTO PATH OF ONCOMING TRAIN and each word transports me into the barren halls of the hospital where smoke hung, a tantalizing noose as we shuffled feet to stiff to lift. We labored on legs that barely moved beneath the encumbrance of cure.

I see you still, strapped to that bed in the *Quiet Room*, your screams bleeding through the small gash between the floor and the door, as if your pain slithered across the old scuffed tile and wrapped itself like vines around my ankles. I've never walked it off.

I admit back then I envied you your open rage, I, who crept past the nurses' station to watch the fury move in waves through your body, lift you off that cot. I'd spent years waging a silent war on my own body. I spoke a lonely language of starvation and celebration, of ounce and scrap, one even I did not understand.

Today this article will creep into the hands of housewives, lawyers, bricklayers, tell them you were valedictorian, class president, a good girl. Will any of them question what would make a girl like you take such a flight? If they wonder they will only whisper.

Tomorrow the news of your death will line the bottoms of bird cages, protect flooring from paint splatter, and I'll wake up and begin forgetting again.

Dear Daryl,

For the first time in two decades I'm in Alabama, where I spent the depths of my longest winter. Almost every day the Mobile sky spilled a cool rain across the campus as I grappled with specters of my childhood. You tried so hard to save me, with Christ, with Camus, with conversation. I fought to find that invincible summer you spoke of but the Thorazine was unforgiving. My hands shook and my thoughts thickened with the rigid stupor of sanity. From my dorm room we watched tentacles of frost creep across the windows in late January. You assured me spring was coming, that daffodils lie dormant beneath a fortress of frost-covered soil. We moved through substance, over dark earth, always toward something I could not see. The books they gave me were unyielding, my eyes moved awkwardly across the pages but nothing seemed to stick. Facts crept constantly away from me, tangents, amendments, tectonic plates constantly shifting beneath me. Only Plath and Sexton could pierce the fog. *One year in every ten I manage it.* Eager to still the storm inside I swallowed a fistful of pills, drifted into the breathless menace of a broken will. How could you salvage a soul like mine?

When I arrived days later, back home, to pace the hospital ward, the wake of your unfamiliar goodness rippled over me. The doctors, those shadowy prophets, took up the burden of my wild winter. Broke the expanse of ice, thawed my cold corpse, dissolved my dark heart to tinder, surely you saw it all along, a word, a world, a way from there to here.

Absolution

Forgive the blackbird,
the creek that splits the stone.
Forgive the timber train
that rattles you from sleep,
the dark air's demon tongue.

Forget the lovely boy
you mistook for salvation.
Forget his body tubular and hard
against your summer skin,
the way the lake glared up
at the hovering moon.

Begin again, embrace
the shattered glass, the sin
and shame of vulgar games,
let the slow gravel stares
fade from your memory.

Forgive the fence, the wind,
the azaleas that refused to grow.
Forget fifteen, its warbling song,
its deep caves of perpetual change.
Begin again at forty, at fifty, now.
Embrace the snug rumor of redemption.

Correspondence

I've written my name on your body,
etched each letter across your back
while you, silent and strong,
embraced the damage.

What those cool blue curtains have seen
as I labored over your belly-
The stiff brown curve of your spine.

Moonlight moaned in that small room,
stars shed tears on our skin.

Through you I wrote my screed to survival.

Transformed into my treatise to childhood trauma,
you bore each lament I wove into muscle,
never spoke the secrets my hands
sutured in your shoulders.

What scars do those walls still hide?
The redemption of spackle and sanding
Fresh paint can't cover it all.

Sunbeams surge through streaked windows,
dust pirouettes across each yellowing page.

Our story an idle rumor adrift in the attic.

Elegy for Anorexia

Say I was a madman who indulged
in honeyed speech,
a woman who never once
arrived on time. Tell them I spent
a lifetime trying but could not explain myself.

I have told myself that virtue
made me vulnerable,
that a girl like me,
always engaged in deceiving
herself, sings old poems to life.
Life doesn't listen.

I lived with a hand hovering over flame
and learned to find the beauty in burns.
I was a barefoot nomad, a renegade dancing
in her own shadow.

I taught my tongue to cradle and to cut.
Once I was harmless, but I vanished
paper thin and hollow into a mirror
I could never please.

Letter to Marilyn

Sometimes you will lament a lost friend you never had. The husky crags of the faces you only barely knew before they disappeared into the ebb and flow of daily life. The ones I always wish I knew are the women who have the power to turn their stares to shrapnel. The ones who work the machinery of their hips like a cyclone drawing all around them in. It is strange mischief the way some women warp the world beneath them. Wilderness rises around them, bird and bush sprawl across the skyline to watch them walk. In their tears a black boon rises. I have never been one of these.

I envy you your evocations of lip and eyelash, your tongue of fire spinning everything to kindling. But yours is a broken country, a kingdom built on the steep embankment of a river that flows wildly, lapping at the soft soil that lines its bed. Yours is the swell and shivering kiss of flood eroding baseboard, of liquid leaking into basement. Your faith, like sedge, is mired in misstep.

Girls like me are rosehips, orchids, variegated flowers vulgarly ordinary. We feign cool indifference; bring fruit salad to family gatherings, fearful to explore the savage continents inside us. We are empty doorway and rotting maple leaf. Drone and jangle of key and complaint, we trudge across kitchens, climb the steep paths of empty rooms; hear almost nothing but the throb of twisted wings just beyond the scrutinizing pane of glaring glass.

These Dreams

In sleep she returns,
still seven, still carrying the broken
pieces of my past in her arms.

My heart hurries to greet her
to hide her from the sinful moon
he crept beneath, to sing into her
peace and poetry,

but my tongue is still bound in barbed wire.

Outside the willow dances
woefully in the breeze.
I think again of my mother,
the sadness squatting inside her,
the solace she did not have to offer.

Some nights they swim circles
in my dreams, their greedy cries
for redemption shuddering
through the years I've spent
silencing them.

Midnight cloaks the world in a semblance of sorrow.

In the blackness I learned the art
of lonesomeness, stretched my arms
across that bed and gasped for breath
in a desert of indifference.

On the nights she returns,
I cannot comfort her.
Shock still shivers across her body.
and I can offer her no safety,

as she drowns in her untenable truth.

The Arsonist's Lament

It was a pleasure to burn
—Ray Bradbury

Night spins us into its spongy palms
with the kind of certitude that leads us
into the uncharted territories of ourselves.

This is the trick of darkness, the mirror
game of midnight, to lure us into believing
we can master it until it spreads,
like a slow fire across the acreage of our lives burning
mile after mile until every inch of us is gone.

In the embers you may find yourself
simple black soot awaiting the house's return
like me, reduced to cinders and the land you built
on, a wasteland of what you could and should
and didn't do.

Thinking of My Father

With a thundering outstretched hand
he strains not to see me.
I am twelve, the woman trapped
in my lanky frame had only just begun
to scratch her way through skin and bone.
That summer I began to dream of boys
Whose slender bodies filled doorways,
cast shadows on the asphalt court,
others thick at the shoreline,
cool to the touch.

All summer I snuck off to sip stolen beer,
smoke bummed cigarettes,
slide myself across smooth bodied boys.
These are the stories that etched lines
across his brow, this is the tale of how
a body breaks beneath a child's weight,
wears thin against another's impulse.

Now, as I've begun to fracture,
bones fissuring beneath my own son's
implosion, my father transforms slowly.
I begin to redefine my past as my son pressed
 past me, through the door,
out into the bitter dark.

Dear Monica,

It's April again. The only plant I haven't killed rises rebelliously at the edge of the yard. Your forsythia raises its vivid yellow blossoms. Do you remember the year we ambled through the nursery, you painstakingly choosing plants that bloom in shade while I plunked roses, marigolds, and sunflowers in the cart? I refused to listen, spent weeks prolonging their demise with water, with food, with the sharp sting of pruning scissors. I lost them all. But that forsythia, it survived the way you swore it would. I try to picture you, halfway round the world, Russian bulky on your tongue, as you haggle in the markets. I fail every time. I am selfish.

The boys are big. The past expands and contracts with the hammering strength of their wills. Once they were the conductors of my days, baseball games, school plays, but the wrench and release of teenage life are slowly taking them from me. It will not be long now until they dissipate into adulthood. I'm sure your boys must be the same. Do you stand outside their bedroom doors and think of the wind coiling through windows? Of the dreams that must surely fill their sleep? Do you recall those distant memories of them, at eight or ten, bike wheels spinning over asphalt, waving as they went? Does your body feel like bursting when you think of them traversing the setting sun? Do you still wake up some nights and find your hand shielding your eyes as if from the glare, as if watching could assure their safety?

Anyway, I miss you and I thought you'd like to know that forsythia still blooms at the road's edge, that even though I've often neglected it, it endures.

How the Light Gets In

First, there must be fissure,
a trembling hand, a sloping step,
a heart clenching tightly in a chest.

Imperfection must crack open
the door.
This will be painful.

No one, including you
escapes the abrupt
quake of things dividing.

What took years to assemble
dissolves instantly.

The floor of your bedroom
opens, a chasm consumes
the man who, for years,
drove your demons down
with his body's tender sway.

You must believe the earth
will treat him gently,
that beyond the lacerating
shadows, light erupts
to lead him.

**Upon Reading That the Gene That Causes Night Owls
Is Called Cry1**

Even our genes are spun into a misty
crystal for cover of starshine and ink blot.
On the deepest levels we turn from sun,
beg for another hour's reprieve from light.

Now even science must acknowledge this;
that we, who find ourselves acquainted so
with the hours after midnight, we're born exploring
the depths of the day's beginning and its end.

We are the silent, sobbing or in celebration,
usher others through the lands to which we are natives.
Come into the alley of the morning, into the small crevice
between what you were and what
you are becoming.

In The Devil's Churn

The wrath of waves has eroded the shoreline
and their rage spins into song.
Atop slick rock I listen to the sea
slicing its way into stone.

Is this a lamentation or a love song?

Green water whips itself to foam
that fills clefted bluffs.
From my stilled lips a prayer for redemption
falls silently into the froth.

The sea baits me with its broken melody.

Peace subsists above wailing water.
The surging, splintering sea raises
its fingers almost to the soles of my feet.
Its grasping hands summon me to stillness.

Must the earth always absorb us?

On the surf, a slick feathered loon,
its blackness sparkling amidst the spray,
rides the furious pitch and roil, submerges,
breaks the surface with a silvery fish.

I, too, have been nourished in chaos.

My god rides the sea's restless back,
curls himself into a salty fist, she must swirl
on a tongue of kelp, but will emerge
on the wings of a lost loon, because
what has been riven must rise.

Letter to David after Visiting the Grand Canyon

Perhaps you're right and faith is a fairy tale, a myth spun over centuries into manacles for the mind. Perhaps men cowering in the stony mouths of caves saw something sinister in the dark clouds that drove back the sun. Maybe the sight of lightning setting the bush ablaze birthed a god conceived in terror. Have we filled the centuries with ceremony to construct certitude? The supply is still so small.

Men have whittled wood and stone, carved idols over ages to beat back the chaos always eager to envelop them, worked their hands raw assembling cathedrals ornamented with one god or another to keep control. At times faith has fed on flesh, devolved to fatwas of war, pogroms, inquisitions, became enamored of the rack, the screw, the bomb. Why is belief so often sustained in slaughter? It all begins and end in blood, does it?

You call faith foolish, say the wise embrace entropy, worship beaker and flask, insist all the truths we seek are secreted into the folds of science. You exhort me to trust the mind, that maze of synapses, your electric gray- matter god. For years I bowed at the altar of intellect, worshipped the book, the blade, the body. Still, like all gods, she is flawed. The cool stone of her cathedral also sticky with the blood of syphilitic sharecroppers, sterilized second-class citizens, patients pacified by Moniz's slice.

I stand on the edge, the earth, an angry mother tears herself in two beneath my feet. I skirt the lip of stone that has given way to water. Even if it is a flaw, a fallacy, here in the arid jaws of the desert I find all the signs of science, all the substantiation I need of God.

Revelations

Perhaps tomorrow the clouds will crack open
and a murky sky will cleave at the horizon
but today the hands of god are at the ends
of a homeless man's arms as he strokes the soil
into small circles,

sifting the silt loose from his own greedy grasp.
He undoes his handiwork in a furious
maelstrom that encircles him,
and in a whirligig of dust, baptizes himself.

The billboard hovering above him
urges passersby to repent,
the day of judgment nears,
Exit here.

Pluvial

Sometimes the sky stares down
with the eye of an angry artist.
In torrents its hands pound hillside
until the earth yields to deluge.

Houses will fold into the avalanche
of soil, bury men beneath the muck,
this is the cost of genius,
the artist cannot afford to care.

Other days the sky, that gentle mother,
will stroke the fields with moisture:
trees will offer up their fruit,
crops will grow, a child will stomp
through puddles in a dance of praise.

Tomorrow the oceans will heave
themselves up and then away
from heaven. Clouds will suckle
on river, lake, and sea.

The rain will run in rivulets
over asphalt into gutters.
The soil will open greedy lips.
Blades of grass will welcome
droplet's gliding down
their supple spines.

That Invincible Summer

In the depth of winter, I finally learned that within me there lay
an invincible summer.
—Albert Camus

You find it in the tentacles of frost
That cling to the window you peer
in late January.
In the yard, there are no signs of Spring,
daffodils lie dormant beneath a faulty fortress
of frozen soil.
Unbroken beneath the expanse of ice
 that hides the still-swaying lake
where soundless fish wait for the warmth
their stilled gills know will come.

Bridget Gage-Dixon has had a life-long love affair with poetry that began with rewriting nursery rhymes and fairytales. She progressed to having her poems included in *Poet Lore, Inkwell, The Cortland Review,* and several other journals. She lives in New Jersey where she teaches and dotes on her grandchildren.

www.ingramcontent.com/pod-product-compliance
Lightning Source LLC
LaVergne TN
LVHW041328080426
835513LV00008B/632